Contents

Why An Attitude Of Gratitude?

God **saved** me

God **keeps** me

God **wins** for me

God **blesses** me

God **frees** me

God **heals** my past

God **leads** me

God is **with** me

God is **for** me

God **loves** me

God **disciplines** me

God **speaks** to me

God **hears** me

God **equips** me

God **empowers** me
God **employs** me
God **fights** for me
God **sings** over me
God **provides** for me
God **calms** me
God **comforts** me
God **rewards** me
God **warns** me
God **protects** me
God **counsels** me
God **advocates** for me
God is **joy** for me
God **sends** me
God **prays** for me
God is all we **need**

The Healing Power Of Gratitude

In the late 1800's, a man named George Mueller operated an orphanage that at one time housed over 1,000 orphans. One morning there was no food to eat, but he called all the children and staff together and prayed thanking God for the provision of food, even though no food was on the table. A few moments later a baker knocked on the door. He told Mr. Muller that God had led him to bake bread the night before and give it to the orphanage. Before the bread was given to the children, a milkman knocked on the door. He said that his milk truck had broken down and he wanted to give the milk to the orphanage. *George Muller gave thanks, even when it took faith to do so.* **Source: *The Expeditionary Man*, Rich Wagner**

There is something about gratitude and graciousness that binds a person to another. Thankful people are contagious creatures and we can also say with assurance that negative people are as well. Thankfulness and gratitude seem to be a lost art in today's world. The something for nothing generation has sprung upon us and too often we fail to take the time to see our blessings and why we have them.

In 1860, the *Lady Elgin* was rammed by the *Augusta* and sank in Lake Michigan near Evanston, Illinois. A ministerial student named Edward Spencer waded again and again into the frigid waters to rescue passengers. In the process, his health was permanently damaged. Some years later at his funeral, it was noted that not one of the people he rescued ever thanked him. **Source: *Disasters, Accidents, and Crises in American History*, Ballard C. Campbell**

That seems to be the swan song of a deteriorating culture, but it seems like there is abundant room for those who wish to be gracious and thankful. Gratitude has a healing power that we can never measure. Study after study confirms that positive, gracious people are far more happier and content than the rest. Why is that? We will explore that more deeply throughout this book.

But I want to go a step further and it certainly is a welcome journey and that is – Christian people have the potential to be the most gracious and thankful people on the planet. Why is that you ask? Well, that really is the content we wish to discover in the pages ahead.

One of the most haunting stories in the gospel account is the saga of the ten lepers that came to Jesus broken and needy. Leprosy in those days (and even today) was almost a death sentence not only physically but more importantly – relationally. They were shunned, quarantined and otherwise rejected by society. Jesus was in many respects, there only hope for a change.

Dr. Luke records the story of this Jesus and lepers encounter and watch the dynamic of all of it. (**Luke 17:11-19 ESV**)

On the way to Jerusalem he was passing along between Samaria and Galilee. 12 And as he entered a village, he was met by ten lepers, who stood at a distance 13 and lifted up their voices, saying, "Jesus, Master, have mercy on us." 14 When he saw them he said to them, "Go and show yourselves to the priests." And as they went, they were cleansed. 15 Then one of them, when he saw that he was healed, turned back, praising God with a loud voice; 16 and he fell on his face at Jesus' feet, giving him thanks. Now he was a Samaritan. 17 Then Jesus answered, "Were not ten cleansed? Where are the nine? 18 Was no one found to return and give praise to God except this foreigner?" 19 And he said to him, "Rise and go your way; your faith has made you well."

What a story. Jesus is ten for ten. Not unusual by any stretch. Not one of the lepers that solicited Jesus goes home the same way they came. What a miracle. What a relief for those who have been disenfranchised for so long. What a gift that is given and the results of this gift would play out for decades to come. You and I would undoubtedly write this story differently if we wrote it. But in this story, God paints a true picture of humanity and far too often a true portrait of – **the Christian church.** Let me explain.

This is a story that is both sad and telling on so many levels, isn't it? First, **it is sad because this great miracle work of Jesus is perceived as a mere "yawn as we go handout" by the nine**, rather than seen as a lifechanging hand up and an avalanche of divine grace freely poured out. Unfortunately, this mentality is alive and not so well even these many centuries later. It is no secret that the children of Israel often lost their way because they suffered from spiritual amnesia. I am afraid we as God's people are far to often like the Israelites. God pours it on in our lives and we barely have time to attend the fellowship or the prayer meeting to follow.

Secondly, **the ten percent return on the work of Jesus is often customary of what we can expect in our churches.** The oft stated phrase bears repeating: "20% of the people do 80% of the work" in most churches. No matter how hard leaders hit this malady, it still seems to hover around that number and if the truth be told, Jesus's earthly ministry results are not a whole lot better. Now let me be clear that Jesus has the divine ability to get all ten on board in this story. But it is the hardness of the heart of man that is at play here. Mankind is often waiting for someone else to do it and often is interested in a "free lunch" to boot.

The Healing Power Of Gratitude is exactly
what it says. It transforms the one who is thankful, and it breeds a culture and community of gracious people. Christians ought to be the most grateful people on this terrestrial ball.

I believe that when you have finished this book, you will be a new and glad proponent of spreading this indispensable wealth that is called "divine gratitude." The best is yet to come, and the half has not yet been told. But in this book. some of it will be uncovered and it is a joy to be a small help in this pearl of great price called thankfulness.

Blessings All Day From The Throne Room,
Chris J. Gregas

God SAVED me....

"Who saved us and called us to a holy calling, not because of our works but because of his own purpose and grace, which he gave us in Christ Jesus before the ages began." 2 Timothy 1:9 ESV

We can never be found if we first don't see that we are lost. That is the power behind the phrase, God saves me. God knew we could never reach His lofty and holy level so he, in time and space, donned an earth suit and paid a debt that we could never pay because of our wretched condition. He came down to our level. Salvation can be seen as being delivered, rescued or spared. When a person is drowning, a rescue or intervention must be done. Now the lifeguard must not only be willing to save but also able to do so. If one of these is missing, the drowning victim will have the ocean for their watery grave.

Jesus is not only able to rescue us from our sin problem, but He is willing to do so for whoever calls on the name of the Lord will be saved. Jesus saves us by dying in our place as a substitute. In the person of Jesus Christ, God sacrificed Himself on our behalf, paying the infinite and eternal penalty only He could pay for us. He rescued us from Hell and placed us on a path that leads to Heaven. Praise His great Name!

Gratitude Corner. Tell God what you are thinking and feeling based on what you have discovered in this reading. Tell someone else about it too. Remember you are in the "Import/Export" business/ministry.

Applications to "God SAVED me" and scriptural support:

- *If you are truly saved, then you should be bearing fruit. (Jn. 15:1-10)*
- *If you are truly saved, then you should be telling others. (2 Cor. 5:14-21)*

God KEEPS me....

"Who by God's power are being guarded through faith for a salvation ready to be revealed in the last time" I Peter 1:5 ESV

The God who saves is the God who keeps and guards. The great shepherd has never lost a sheep yet and He will not start with you. It is the work of the Father to select and choose. It is the work of the Son to save and rescue. It is the blessed work of the Holy Spirit to seal and secure every believer of every age forever. Isn't it wonderful to know that God has the ability and desire to keep us until "that day?" That His goal is for us to safely reach the shores of Heaven which is our real Home and final resting place? As a believer in Jesus, we are promised a new life covered under the protection of God in which NOTHING can separate us from His love.

"But the Lord is faithful, and he will strengthen you and protect you from the evil one", says Paul Jesus reminds us who are His sheep, *"I give them eternal life, and they shall never perish; no one will snatch them out of my hand. My Father, who has given them to me, is greater than all; no one can snatch them out of my Father's hand. I and the Father are one."* Praise the great Name of Jesus for keeping us saved.

Gratitude Corner. Tell God what you are thinking and feeling based on what you have discovered in this reading. Tell someone else about it too. Remember you are in the "Import/Export" business/ministry.

Applications to **"God KEEPS me"** and scriptural support:

- *If you are truly safe, then it should be seen in how you live. (Eph. 1:13-21)*
- *If you are truly safe, then guilt or shame should be gone from your walk. (Rom. 8:1-4)*

God WINS for me....

"No, despite all these things, overwhelming victory is ours through Christ, who loved us." Romans 8:37 NLT

Winning has to be one of the greatest feelings in the universe. Being party to a victory is a feeling that captures our heart and mind like no other. The Bible is clear about this: God is willing to fight for His child. To fight for His people. All thorough out the Older Testament, we see a God that fought for His people. The phrase, "the battle is the Lord's" is repeated in some fashion all throughout is 39 books. At the end of the age, God in Christ, will fight for His children and people as He vanquishes every enemy at the last great human battle on earth. (i.e. Rev. 20:1-ff)

We are winners in Christ not because of our work or effort but because of His. The cross was the crusher over all Satanic powers and the dark world was once for all defeated. (Col. 2:14-15; Heb. 2:14-15; I Jn. 3:8) Even though Satan and his minions have been served and are waiting final placement, they still (out on bail) have delegated power to sully the waters of our body and soul but make no mistake about it: We are more than **WINNERS** through Him who loved us. End of story. Walk in it and be a blessing.

Gratitude Corner. Tell God what you are thinking and feeling based on what you have discovered in this reading. Tell someone else about it too. Remember you are in the "Import/Export" business/ministry.

Applications to "God WINS for me" and scriptural support:

- *If you are a winner in Christ, walk in such a way that Satan and man know you are. (2 Cor. 5:6-9)*
- *If you are winner in Christ, realize that you are not fighting **FOR** victory but **FROM** victory. (Col. 2:14-15; Heb. 2:14-15)*

God BLESSES me....

"Blessed be the God and Father of our Lord Jesus Christ, who has blessed us with every spiritual blessing in the heavenly places in Christ," Ephesians 1:3 NASB

You have undoubtedly heard the phrase, *"To blessed to be stressed."* Now in a perfect world we would live like this all day long but, we often forget that the blessings of God work for us even when life is not. The problem is not found in the statement but with us. We are ever challenged with the goal to live not for what we may get from God but from all that He has given us already. The law says, *"Do and be blessed. Grace says, "You are blessed, therefore do."* The verse says we have been blessed not we will be blessed. We no longer are called to be beggars but appropriators. Claiming what has already been deposited into our spiritual account. That is the secret of victorious Christian living. **How are you doing in this area?**

Peter tells us that we have all we need for living and for godly living through the work of Christ on the cross. Gratitude for these facts ought to be the hallmark of our mind and heart. To be chosen, selected, drawn, justified and secured for a final destination place called Heaven is more than we can ever understand or fully appreciate.

Gratitude Corner. Tell God what you are thinking and feeling based on what you have discovered in this reading. Tell someone else about it too. Remember you are in the "Import/Export" business/ministry.

Applications to "God BLESSES me" and scriptural support:

- *If you are completely spiritually blessed, then there is no excuse on why you can't live the Christian life successfully. (2 Peter 1:3-4)*

God FREES me....

"So, if the Son sets you free, you will be free indeed." John 8:36 ESV

Is there anything more wonderful and fulfilling than being spiritually free? I guess if it is never been a reality in your life then you can probably think of a lot of other things that seemingly bring fulfillment and pleasure. But Paul reminds us that it was for spiritual freedom itself that Christ set us free. In other words, Christ wants us to be free, but He wants to experience in all of its beauty. Maybe that explains why Satan and his minions fight us so hard at this point because they know that spiritual freedom is a passion and addiction that is hard to break once it is in full swing.

What a gracious work of God to not only free us from sin positionally but in a practical way all throughout our Christian lives. (Rom. 6:1-14) And if that isn't enough, we are promised that we will be loosed one day from the very presence of sin when we step across Heaven's shores. If that doesn't bring a gratitude to your heart that results in a smile to your face, then maybe you need to ask the Lord to get you back into the land of the living. Free indeed is what we need when all is said and done. It is available only through the cross work of Jesus Christ. Are you free on the inside? Are you enslaved to Jesus Christ or are you enslaved to your own tangled web of sin and shame? Do you long to be free practically (daily and personally) speaking? This freedom is yours for the asking and receiving

Gratitude Corner. Tell God what you are thinking and feeling based on what you have discovered in this reading. Tell someone else about it too. Remember you are in the "Import/Export" business/ministry.

Applications to "**God FREES me**" and scriptural support:

- *You will be practically free in Christ as you continue in His Word and abide in Christ. (Jn. 8:31-36)*

God HEALS my past....

"Brothers, I do not consider that I have made it my own. But one thing I do: forgetting what lies behind and straining forward to what lies ahead." Phil. 3:13

I learned along time ago something that literally changed the direction of my life forever. What was it? It was based on the verse that is before us. Here's what I learned and what you must learn and if you do, your gratitude meter will shoot up like a rocket and it will float securely the rest of your days. **Here it is: *Learn from the past but do not (for a minute) live in it.*** It is a simple statement but profound on so many levels. How many of God's people live with their past unresolved? They are driving through this life using the rearview mirror to direct their steps and occasionally, they are party to a crash.

The reason our gratitude meter is always at the bottom is because while we make two steps forward in our spiritual growth, our past paralyzes us time and time again and we go back five steps. If you want to know the key to joy and advancement as a Christian, you must allow the Lord to resolve and heal your past. No pain, no gain. If you continue to bury your trash and stink, do not be surprised that on some certain day, you must deal with it again and this time, it will be worse than ever. Healing is available in Christ. Why do we continue to stay sick and rundown spiritually when there is an Answer within us?

Gratitude Corner. Tell God what you are thinking and feeling based on what you have discovered in this reading. Tell someone else about it too. Remember you are in the "Import/Export" business/ministry.

Applications to "God HEALS my past" and scriptural support:

- *When God heals my past, I will forget (not count on) what has happened before and look forward to what lies ahead. (2 Cor.5:17)*

God LEADS me....

"He calls his own sheep by name and leads them out. After he has gathered his own flock, he walks ahead of them, and they follow him because they know his voice." John 10:3-4 NLT

God is in the business of leading people. That means He want to lead and guide – YOU! It doesn't matter where you have come from or even where you are going but it does matter on who leads you and who YOU follow. We can be thankful everyday that the God of the universe has time for us and promises to take the special time to show us the way in which we should go. When God bolts the door, don't try to get in through the window. That is never wise.

God leads us and we follow. That reminds us who we are not what we are trying to be. We are His sheep in His pasture, and He will feed us and lead us as long as we report for duty. The believer often comes to some dark passage, or encounters some severe trial, which so overshadows the way that he fears to go forward lest he fall. But when he clasps the hand of his Heavenly Father, he is led gently over the rough and dangerous places and landed safely in some secure spot. The storms may rage, and angry waves threaten to engulf, but if we keep our eyes on Jesus, we shall outride the storms successfully. Amen.

Gratitude Corner. Tell God what you are thinking and feeling based on what you have discovered in this reading. Tell someone else about it too. Remember you are in the "Import/Export" business/ministry.

Applications to **"God LEADS me"** and scriptural support:

- *When you are led by God, you simply follow Him. (Jn. 10: 3-4)*
- *When you are led by God, you will be a source of spiritual influence and wisdom to others. (Is. 58:11)*
- *When you are led by God, you will not walk in the flesh. (Gal. 5:16-25)*

God is WITH me....

"I will never leave you or forsake you, says the Lord." Hebrews 13:5 (KJV)

One of the things that brings little children great anxiety is a storm outside. Because they do not understand the machinery of storms, they often believe that their lives and the lives of all those around them is in great peril even if it is just raining hard. But one thing is for sure, when Mom or Dad comes into the room while all is breaking loose outside, a calmness seems to suddenly grip the young child. Has anything changed outside? Probably not but one thing has changed: **Someone has come to be with the child and that chases away the fear and dread.** David said it best when he wrote, *"though I walk through the valley of deep shadows, I will fear no evil because – YOU (My Shepherd) are with me."* (Psalm 23:4) God's manifest presence!

We can be ever grateful that what is a danger all around us is struck down and put the flight because of WHO is within us. Peace comes not from the absence of trouble, but from the presence of God. Max Lucado reminds us. *"Don't equate the presence of God with a good mood or a pleasant temperament. God is near whether you are happy or not."* Listen: When you can't see God's hand in a matter, trust His heart and always remember, that He will guide you until death.

Gratitude Corner. Tell God what you are thinking and feeling based on what you have discovered in this reading. Tell someone else about it too. Remember you are in the "Import/Export" business/ministry.

Applications to **"God is WITH me"** and scriptural support:

- *When I know God is with me, I will not fear what man can do to me. (Rom. 8:31)*
- *When I know God is with me, I can do what God has called me to do in reaching the world for Christ. (Matt. 28:18-20)*

God is FOR me....

"If God is for me, who can be against me." Romans 8:31 ESV

One of the toughest things in life to endure is when people are actively against us and they are voicing their opposition clearly. Jesus told us to love our enemies and we are reminded that He had plenty so we will have our share too – sometimes right in the same household or family. There are days when we feel that the whole world is against us. That nothing is going right and the mistake we made today was merely getting up.

In **Romans 8:31-39**, Paul gives us (4) reasons why we can say that God is for us and if He is for us, who can stand against us and win.

First Reason: God will give us all things. (8:32) If He gave us His "best" gift than how shall He not give us the gifts we need to live daily among our critics.
Second Reason: No one can bring a spiritual charge against us. (8:33)   ***Third Reason***: No one can condemn us to Hell. (8:34)
Last Reason: No one can separate us from the love of Christ. (8:35-39) Christ loves us, and no enemy or weapon or calamity can separate us from the love of God in Christ Jesus our Lord.

Gratitude Corner. Tell God what you are thinking and feeling based on what you have discovered in this reading. Tell someone else about it too. Remember you are in the "Import/Export" business/ministry.

<u>Applications</u> to **"God is FOR me"** and scriptural support:

- *If God is for me, He will graciously give me what I need. (Rom. 8:32)*
- *If God is for me, He will not bring a charge against me. (Rom. 8:33)*
- *If God is for me, He will not condemn me in life or to Hell. (Rom. 8:34)*
- *If God is for me, nothing could ever separate me from His love. (Rom. 8:35-39)*

God LOVES me....

"For God showed His love for us in that while we were still sinners, Christ died for us." Romans 5:8 ESV

God's love for us in Christ is off the chain when you think about it. His love can be briefly stated as His willingness to act in our best interest, especially in meeting our greatest need, even though it cost Him everything and even though we were the least worthy of such love. Wow! In a world where love seems to be shrinking in its scope and value, God shows His love for lost and desperate sinners. If that isn't love. If that doesn't spur a hear of gratitude than we must look and see if we have been true recipients of His work.

C.S. Lewis reminds us *"Though our feelings come and go, God's love for us does not."* Are you not glad you know this? Thankfulness in our heart springs from knowing how God feels about us though we know He does not have to feel this way at all. **(Zephaniah 3:17)** In this cold and merciless world, many people fall in and out of love and change their mind like the winds change direction, but God's love is not wavering or dependent upon our actions or circumstance. He loves in spite of. He loves on the front end His people and our task is to love Him back and love others.

Gratitude Corner. Tell God what you are thinking and feeling based on what you have discovered in this reading. Tell someone else about it too. Remember you are in the "Import/Export" business/ministry.

Applications to **"God LOVES me"** and scriptural support:

- *Since God loves me unconditionally, I can rest in my eternal security that is free from God's wrath. (Rom. 5:6-10; Eph. 1:4-5)*
- *Since God loves me unconditionally, we can freely and powerfully love others no matter who they are. (I Jn. 3:16-20)*
- *Since God loves me, I do not have to give in to fear. (I Jn. 4:18)*

God DISCIPLINES me....

"Do not regard lightly the discipline of the Lord, nor be weary when reproved by him. For the Lord disciplines the one he loves and chastises everyone whom he receives." Hebrews 12:5-6 ESV

Pastor John MacArthur writes, "The discipline of the Lord comes for three reasons. Number one, **Retribution**. Number two, **Prevention**. And number three, **Education**. There is a sense in which God disciplines us when we sin. It is not redemptive discipline, it is corrective. ***But it is retribution***. We sin, and we get disciplined. We can be grateful for that because we need to remember that sin brings death and pain in any person's life. When God uses discipline in a corrective and punishment way, it is for our good and deeper holiness. (Heb. 12:10) The second reason goes a little deeper. Did you know that sometimes God disciplines us not as a result of sin, but to keep us from sinning? ***That is preventative***. This can come in a variety of ways, but we need to know that God wants to warn us and keep us from ruining our lives and the lives of others so He will bring out the paddle in some form. Lastly, some things in your life are just to teach you and educate you to what is real. God wants us to know that He is enough for what we need – period and He wants us to share that with others in word and through what we have learned to put to work in our lives. ***That is education*** in the school of Christ and its graduation rates are extremely high.

Gratitude Corner. Tell God what you are thinking and feeling based on what you have discovered in this reading. Tell someone else about it too. Remember you are in the "Import/Export" business/ministry.

<u>**Applications** to "**God DISCIPLINES me**" and scriptural support:</u>

- *Because God disciplines us, it proves that we are His children. (Heb. 12:4-11)*
- *Because God disciplines us, He will impart wisdom. (Prov. 13:24)*

God SPEAKS to me....

"My sheep hear my voice, and I know them, and they follow me. I give them eternal life, and they will never perish, and no one will snatch them out of my hand." -John 10:27-28 ESV

God is still in the **SPEAKING** business. Now we can say with relative certainty that God speaks **primarily and chiefly** – through the Word of God, the Bible. (2 Tim. 3:16-17) God also speaks to us in this age by or through His Son. (Heb. 1:1-2) But His Son, the living Word never says things to us that contradict the written Word. Romans 1:20 says that God speaks to us through our varied circumstances whatever they may be. He is working all things together for our good and His glory. (Rom. 8:28) God speaks to us through His Spirit (John 14:17) but we are told to test the spirits and to remind ourselves that the Holy Spirit will never contradict the written Word – never. God is speaking to us constantly but are we listening? We can be thankful a million times over that the Creator – is interested in communicating with us.

In His parable of the "Good Shepherd and His Sheep" Jesus taught, *"The gatekeeper opens the gate for him, and the sheep listen to his voice. He calls his own sheep by name and leads them out. When he has brought out all his own, he goes on ahead of them, and his sheep follow him, because they know his voice."* (John 10: 3-5)

Gratitude Corner. Tell God what you are thinking and feeling based on what you have discovered in this reading. Tell someone else about it too. Remember you are in the "Import/Export" business/ministry.

<u>**Applications** to **"God SPEAKS to me"** and scriptural support:</u>

- *God speaks to me in and from His Word, the Bible. (2 Tim. 3:16-17)*
- *God speaks to me through godly counsel. (Prov. 19:20; Rev. 3:16-18)*
- *God speaks through His Spirit in His Word. (Jn. 16:13-15)*

God HEARS me....

"And this is the confidence that we have toward him, that if we ask anything according to his will, he hears us. And if we know that he hears us in whatever we ask, we know that we have the requests that we have asked of him. I John 5:14-15 ESV

God speaks to us. We got it. But do we believe He HEARS us when **WE** speak? Many people ask, Is God too busy to hear me and pay attention to my particular situation? Is He off on other more important things than seeing my circumstance that is eating me alive slowly but surely? Does God hear us when we pray and cry out to Him. Well, we can be eternally grateful and joyful that His Word confirms that He does and does so with great love. There is a "confidence" that John says that we carry because we know that our relationship with Christ is not – one way. How important is it for you to know that God hears you?

1 Peter 3:12 says, "*For the eyes of **the Lord** are on the righteous and his ears are attentive to their prayer, but the face of **the Lord** is against those who do evil.*" Notice that the lost do not have that confidence or promise when they pray or talk to God. **GRATEFUL!** John16:24 says, "Until now you have not asked for anything in my name. Ask and you will receive, and your joy will be complete." God listens and He is ready to answer, all you must do is ask. Could God have made it any easier than that?

Gratitude Corner. Tell God what you are thinking and feeling based on what you have discovered in this reading. Tell someone else about it too. Remember you are in the "Import/Export" business/ministry.

Applications to "God HEARS me" and scriptural support:

- *Because God hears me, He will answer the prayers that I pray. (I Jn. 5:14-15)*
- *Because God hears me, I can be confident that He will communicate His truth to me. (Jer. 33:3)*

God EQUIPS me....

"Now may the God of peace who brought again from the dead our Lord Jesus....equip you with everything good that you may do his will, working in us that which is pleasing in his sight, through Jesus Christ, to whom be glory forever and ever. Amen."
-Hebrews 13:20-21 ESV

The word or idea of *"equip or equipping"* means to completely prepare for a work to do. Another meaning implies "to put someone back completely in joint." It means that God wants to make YOU the PERFECT candidate for His eternal work in someone else's life. I cannot influence someone that God has chiefly called YOU to impact in the same way. I like what Paul says in Ephesians 2:10 when he writes, *"We are His Masterpieces re-created in Christ Jesus to carry out good works which God has beforehand cleared a certain path for certain works for each of us to walk in."*

Aren't you glad that you do not have to bear the brunt of responsibility when it comes to being equipped and ready to serve the Lord? *"Such is the confidence that we have through Christ toward God. Not that we are sufficient in ourselves to claim anything as coming from us, but our sufficiency is from God, who has made us sufficient to be ministers of a new covenant, not of the letter but of the Spirit. (2 Cor. 3:4-6a ESV)* What a grateful heart!

Gratitude Corner. Tell God what you are thinking and feeling based on what you have discovered in this reading. Tell someone else about it too. Remember you are in the "Import/Export" business/ministry.

<u>Applications</u> to "God EQUIPS me" and scriptural support:

- *God equips me to share His gospel with the lost. (2 Cor. 3:3-6)*
- *God equips me to carry out His will in the earth. (Heb. 13:20-21)*
- *God equips me to defeat the world, the flesh and devil. (2 Cor. 10:3-5)*

God EMPOWERS me....

"His divine power has granted to us all things that pertain to life and godliness, through the knowledge of him who called us to his own glory and excellence, by which he has granted to us his precious and very great promises." -2 Peter 1:3-4 ESV

To be empowered to so something is one of the great confidence boosters in life. It is being given the authority to accomplish something and the result is confidence and competence. God has empowered us to do His work. Did you get that? The God of the universe has given us "the goods" to represent Him in the earth. Peter says He has given us all we need to live life and to live life in a godly manner. Sometimes we see our lives or our Christian lives as "deficit" living and that we are in a death struggle to eek out a meaningful existence. But that is not what the scriptures portray. God's promises are yes and amen. They are true and they are trustworthy and when God says that He has given us all that we need to serve Him, we better receive that.

Now to him who is able to do far more abundantly than all that we ask or think, according to the power at work within us, says Paul. No temptation has overtaken you that is not common to man. God is faithful, and he will not let you be tempted beyond your ability, but with the temptation he will also provide the way of escape, that you may be able to endure it. Grateful for the help Lord. I need you.

Gratitude Corner. Tell God what you are thinking and feeling based on what you have discovered in this reading. Tell someone else about it too. Remember you are in the "Import/Export" business/ministry.

Applications to "God EMPOWERS me" and scriptural support:

- *Since God empowers me, I can share the gospel with His power and authority. (Acts 1:8)*
- *Since God empowers me, I can deal with my trials with His grace. (2 Cor. 12:7-10)*

God EMPLOYS me....

"Therefore, my beloved brothers, be steadfast, immovable, always abounding in the work of the Lord, knowing that in the Lord your labor is not in vain." -I Corinthians 15:58 ESV

Isn't it great to be employed? It is no fun being without a job or unable to pay your bills because you lack income. Employment is a must if you are to feel like you are accomplishing something no matter what it is. It is no different in the spiritual realm. Peter reminds us that in his first letter that we are "to employ or serve" others with the gift(s) that God has given us by grace. There is no time or reason why we cannot be employed daily by the Master Employer. He always has gainful employment and to think that He would hire you and me to carry out His work is a scream. Paul reminds us that we are fellow-workers and fellow-team members of Heaven's Enterprise bound for glory!

Today, this moment, come to the realization that you are an important part of the God of the universe's workforce. He could have chosen to go it ALONE, but He chose **YOU** and He gladly did so. He is not ashamed to call you a brother or a sister or a fellow-worker for that matter. (Heb. 2:10) Your labor of love is never in vain because the one who does God's work will get God's pay, some certain hour and some certain day. That is why you can keep on.

Gratitude Corner. Tell God what you are thinking and feeling based on what you have discovered in this reading. Tell someone else about it too. Remember you are in the "Import/Export" business/ministry.

Applications to "God EMPLOYS me" and scriptural support:

- *My work with Christ is a shared work and a shared reward. (I Cor. 3:5-9)*
- *My work for God is built on the strength of serving others. (I Pet. 4:10)*
- *My works for God are ordained and we must walk in them. (Eph. 2:10)*

God FIGHTS for me....

"The eternal God is your dwelling place, and underneath are the everlasting arms. And he thrust out the enemy before you and said, Destroy." -Deuteronomy 33:27 ESV

Isn't it nice when someone stands up for you? How does that make you feel? I can remember as a young teen being bullied by an older teen and my older brother consequently "taking care of business" for me. For him to fight for me and assume the risk was monumental to me and these many years later, I am still writing about it with gladness and gratitude. One of the most wonderful biblical truths that both the Jewish people and Christians have enjoyed through the centuries is the promise that God assumes the responsibility to **FIGHT OUR BATTLES.** "The battle is the Lord's" is a familiar phrase through the Older Testament and the work of Christ on the cross (Col. 2:14-15)

God will fight our battles means we do not have to anguish, be anxious, or be discouraged when bad things happen in our lives. When it seems like our situation is hopeless or the matter at hand is too overwhelming, we may be tempted to doubt God, but He has promised to take care of us. (Philippians 4:19) In this, we can be filled with thankfulness that leads us to great confidence in what God is doing and will do in our lives. Remember, we do not fight **FOR** victory but **FROM** victory. Christ assumes the freight.

Gratitude Corner. Tell God what you are thinking and feeling based on what you have discovered in this reading. Tell someone else about it too. Remember you are in the "Import/Export" business/ministry.

<u>Applications</u> to "God FIGHTS for me" and scriptural support:

- *God fighting for us proves that He is for us and with us every day. (Josh. 1:9)*
- *God fighting for us means that He will take care of those who trouble us. (2 Thess. 1:6)*

God SINGS over me....

"The Lord your God is in your midst, a mighty one who will save; He will rejoice over you with gladness; He will quiet you by his love; He will exult over you with loud singing." -Zephaniah 3:17 ESV

One of the most beautiful scenes in a household is a mother or father singing over or to their little child. It doesn't matter if they can sing. That isn't the point. It is an age-old practice that brings great intimacy and love - to both parent and baby. In a similar but more pronounced fashion, God sings over all of His children and He **CAN SING** and is not afraid to sing loudly and confidently. Just as a loving parent cradles a child and sings out of love, so God's song over His people is born of His great love. After a time of hardship, our loving Lord dries His people's tears, comforts their hearts, and welcomes them into a new world. He gives us this great and precious promises.

"He is in our midst" which means that He is with is and in us so there is no separation between us. Can you say thankful?
"He will rejoice over you with gladness" which implies that God gets charged up over us being His children. How's that for feeling meaningful?
"He will quiet you by His love". This reminds us that no matter what is going all around us, His unconditional, strong love towards us will get us through even the darkest night. What a joy to know and rest in!

Gratitude Corner. Tell God what you are thinking and feeling based on what you have discovered in this reading. Tell someone else about it too. Remember you are in the "Import/Export" business/ministry.

<u>Applications</u> to **"God SINGS over me"** and scriptural support:

- *God singing over me reminds me that I am greatly loved and part of His great family.*

God PROVIDES for me....

"And God is able to make all grace abound to you, so that having all sufficiency in all things at all times, you may abound in every good work." -2 Corinthians 9:8 ESV

Provision. A big word with a big promise. To provide anything means that you have the means to do so. And either out of obligation or because of the pleasure of sheer giving, you provide to someone else something of notable value and assistance. **Think about what God did for us in Christ?** If He never did one more thing for us than redeem us from our sin and selves, it would surely be enough to overflowing. God has always been in the business of providing for His children. In the garden, He provided a covering for Adam and Eve. For Abraham, He provided a ram in the bushes. We can march down through the ages even until today and we see God faithfully providing for His children in big ways. And He has promised to do so and will not fail – ever!

God is fully aware of our needs and the Bible tells us of how God wants us to come to him with every need and care and worry that we may have. *"Consider the birds: they neither plant nor reap, they have neither storehouses nor barns, and yet God feeds them. Of how much more value are you than the birds!" "For the LORD God is a sun and shield; the LORD bestows favor and honor. No good thing does he withhold from those who walk uprightly."* The Lord is your Provider and in that you can rejoice and be forever thankful.

Gratitude Corner. Tell God what you are thinking and feeling based on what you have discovered in this reading. Tell someone else about it too. Remember you are in the "Import/Export" business/ministry.

<u>**Applications** to "**God PROVIDES for me**" and scriptural support:</u>

- *God's provision for me means that all of my needs will be meet in Christ. (Phil. 4:13-19)*
- *God provides faithfully for me because I'm His. (Matt. 7:11)*

God CALMS me....

"Come to me, all who labor and are heavy laden, and I will give you rest." -Jesus, Matthew 11:28 ESV

Rest. How important is that for the weary and tired soul? **Sleep** is a wonderful gift from God on most days. The one who burns the candle on both ends will someday regret it. We need a calmness down in the depths of our soul and the good news is – *Jesus provides that to each of His children.* We seek rest on a vacation. Or watching TV. Or taking a nap. All these things may give us temporary rest but not the kind of rest that we really need. Only Jesus has that stash and He has it in abundance. But the key is: we must go to Him for it. He is willing to give it, but He will not waste on those who will not abide in Him for what they need. Did you hear that? One of the things that I am grateful for is that God in Christ offers and provides me spiritual rest. When all hell is breaking loose in your life, there is a Wonderful Counselor!

He gives what no one else can give. The writer of Hebrews tells us that there is a REST to the people of God and that rest is what all of us can enjoy if we know Christ. I love what the Shepherd of the Psalms, David writes in Psalm 23. *"The LORD is my shepherd; I shall not want. He makes me lie down in green pastures. He leads me beside still waters. He restores my soul. He leads me in paths of righteousness for his name's sake. Even though I walk through the valley of the shadow of death, I will fear no evil, for you are with me..."* Do you need rest today? Christ is your rest if you trust Him.

Gratitude Corner. Tell God what you are thinking and feeling based on what you have discovered in this reading. Tell someone else about it too. Remember you are in the "Import/Export" business/ministry.

<u>Applications to "God CALMS me" and scriptural support:</u>

- *Being calm in God means that I believe in Him and His mighty power. (Ps. 46:10)*
- *Being calm in God means I can run to Him. (Matt. 11:28-30)*

God COMFORTS me....

"Blessed be the God and Father of our Lord Jesus Christ, the Father of mercies and God of all comfort, who comforts us in all our affliction, so that we may be able to comfort those who are in any affliction, with the comfort with which we ourselves are comforted by God." -2 Corinthians 1:3-4 ESV

How important is comfort and encouragement? When we are down and discouraged, a word of comfort and wisdom goes a long way to us getting back on track or through another day. People can be either a comfort or a thorn but not so with God. He is a Comforter extraordinaire for those of us who know Him. He is the SOURCE of all comfort and so to turn to Him when we are down and out is the wisest thing to do. There is no end to God's compassion. His desire and ability to wrap His arms around us are not constrained by circumstances. This understanding fills us with great gratitude because we know that what we need is what will get with our Father.

R.C. Sproul reminds us, *"What is comfort? Comfort means consolation. The idea would be that God comes to console us and bind up our wounds after the battle. While this is true enough, it is not the meaning of the Greek term found in John 14:16. Comfort is derived from the Latin, meaning "with strength." The Comforter comes not to console us after the battle, but with strength and power to fortify us before and in the midst of the battle. Because Jesus has already overcome the world (John 16:33), we can be of good cheer, and we can fight fearlessly as those who are "more than conquerors."*

Gratitude Corner. Tell God what you are thinking and feeling based on what you have discovered in this reading. Tell someone else about it too. Remember you are in the "Import/Export" business/ministry.

<u>**Applications** to "**God COMFORTS me**" and scriptural support:</u>
- *God's comfort comes to us so we can give it away to others. (2 Cor.1:3-11)*

God REWARDS me....

"And you have made them a kingdom and priests to our God, and they shall reign on the earth." -Revelation 5:10 ESV

Have you ever received a reward or an award? How great is that honor for your esteem and feelings of acceptance? Rewards are something to look forward to and you always want to know what you need to do or be to garner them. God has rewarded us with a place in His royal and eternal family. He has made us kings (queens) and priests (those who represent God to man and man to God) and we have the promise that we will one day rule and reign with Christ on the earth.

Eric Celerier writes,"<u>Hebrews 11:6</u> tells us this: "And it is impossible to please God without faith. **Anyone who wants to come to him must believe that God exists** and that he rewards those who sincerely seek him." (NLT) **Believing in God** is the first step. It's believing in His existence, in His salvation through Jesus, His Son. It's believing in forgiveness of sin. It's believing in His grace. **Believing God** is the next step. It's believing in His promises, in His perfect plans for your life, in His unconditional love for you. It's believing before seeing... From this step — coming to God — a **promise** is made. It concerns you in particular, you who believe He exists...You see, **God rewards those who sincerely seek Him.** This word "reward" literally means, in biblical Greek, "one who pays wages." **Believing that He exists is enough for Him to act**. That is the full circle of God rewarding us.

Gratitude Corner. Tell God what you are thinking and feeling based on what you have discovered in this reading. Tell someone else about it too. Remember you are in the "Import/Export" business/ministry.

<u>Applications</u> to <u>"God REWARDS me"</u> <u>and scriptural support:</u>

- *God rewards me for living for Him and pleasing Him. (2 Cor. 5:1-11)*
- *God rewards me for bearing up under persecution. (Lk. 6:22-23)*

God WARNS me....

"For we must all appear before the judgment seat of Christ, so that each one may receive what is due for what he has done in the body, whether good or evil. Therefore, knowing the fear of the Lord, we persuade others...." -2 Corinthians 5:10-11 ESV

How valuable is it when someone warns you of some impending danger? Worth its weight in gold. Warnings on the outside seem to be personal but if they have good intel tied to them, they can literally save our lives and provide a future. God is faithful when it comes to warning His children. From the word of God, the Bible, to godly counsel that can give us a spiritual "heads up" to understanding that someday we are going to give an accounting of our lives after we came to Christ. Now that might seem to be a subject, we are interested in, but we ought to be because we cannot escape it even if we wanted to. We can be eternally grateful to the Lord that He lets us know that there is a **FINAL EXAM** coming and He gives us time to prepare for it or fare better on it someday. That is His wonderful grace and love.

Howard Green asks, *"What will happen to your walk with the Lord if you live each day with the Bema Seat as the starting point and not look at it as something that will occur way off in the distant future? If we really begin to comprehend the amazing rewards and joys Christ has planned for us at His judgment seat, we would be increasingly focused on what brings Him glory and not settle for an apathetic Christian walk."* Aren't you glad that I am writing about this all-important event in this book? You should be. God is.

Gratitude Corner. Tell God what you are thinking and feeling based on what you have discovered in this reading. Tell someone else about it too. Remember you are in the "Import/Export" business/ministry.

<u>Applications</u> to "**God WARNS me**" and scriptural support:

- *God's warning to us who are saved is not about our **sins** but about our **service**. (I Cor. 3:8-15)*

God PROTECTS me....

"The angel of the Lord encamps around those who fear him and delivers them. Oh, taste and see that the Lord is good! Blessed is the man who takes refuge in him!" -Psalm 34:7-8

Protection. That is kind of important to living a life that can go the distance. Without protection, we are terribly vulnerable to all different kinds of enemies that claw at us on a daily basis. The Police, the military and even the very locks on our doors all give us a semblance of peace and safety even in a world that is becoming increasingly violent. God is no slouch in this area of protection. He has promised in so many scriptures to take good care of His own. That does not mean that we will skate through life without harm or hurt but He will preserve us and allow us to enter Heaven's shores, safe and secure. Guardian angels and the providential hand of God are our front and rear guards.

So, we can confidently say, "The Lord is my helper; I will not fear; what can man do to me?" Every word of God proves true; he is a shield to those who take refuge in him. The fear of man lays a snare, but whoever trusts in the LORD is safe. You can take these promises to the bank and God assumes the responsibility of protecting us until it is our time to go to our Real Home. That ought to bring gladness to your heart and an assurance that you are indestructible until God is finished with you. What a way to live – and someday die! Can you say grateful!

Gratitude Corner. Tell God what you are thinking and feeling based on what you have discovered in this reading. Tell someone else about it too. Remember you are in the "Import/Export" business/ministry.

Applications to "God PROTECTS me" and scriptural support:

- *God's protection has to do with guarding us from the devil. (2 Thess. 3:3-5)*
- *God's protection gives us the confidence that nothing that He does not want for us will come to us. (Is. 54:17)*

God COUNSELS me....

There are many plans in a man's heart; nevertheless, the counsel of the Lord, that shall stand. -Proverbs 19:21

We have many plans, don't we? Our lives are made up of activities and pursuits that we believe will bring us happiness and/or others happiness. The truth is, we don't know what I do will hold. We have not been promised anything by our Creator as it relates to our longevity. We live day by day whether we revel in that thought and plan or not. God is in the business of COUNSEL and DIRECTION. Jesus is indeed the "Wonderful Counselor" and He guides us (if that is our desire) in the way of the Father. Are you being led by God on a daily basis? Are you grateful that you can approach the Lord and seek His guidance in a world where darkness and chaos seem to reign supreme? I, like the Psalmist cry, *"I will bless the LORD who gives me counsel."* **(Ps. 16:7)** How about you?

The idea of God counseling us is the idea of Him giving us – **ADVICE**. Like a good parent or a lawyer who we have retained, God is supreme in His mighty and all-knowing advice. We are encouraged to "trust the Lord with all of our hearts and not lean on our own understanding but all of our ways, acknowledge Him and the PROMISE – He will direct our paths." How thankful are you today for the wise counsel of God in His Word? How grateful are you to be connected with the God who knows everything and more? In a world where chaos and darkness reigns, God's own have the wonderful opportunity to hear from God with confidence.

Gratitude Corner. Tell God what you are thinking and feeling based on what you have discovered in this reading. Tell someone else about it too. Remember you are in the "Import/Export" business/ministry.

<u>**Applications** to "God COUNSELS me" and scriptural support:</u>

- *God counsels me in His Word, and I am at peace. (Ps. 119:24)*

God ADVOCATES for me....

"My little children, I am writing these things to you so that you may not sin. But if anyone does sin, we have an advocate with the Father, Jesus Christ the righteous." -I John 2:1

A good Lawyer is a treasure in troubled times. I am always amazed at the job and posture of - defense lawyers. Their job is to their client off or their sentence reduced - even if they are guilty. It is an art that makes them pretty *unique* indeed. Imagine having someone, who you hardly know, advocating for you at the highest level, even if you are guilty. In a similar way, that is what Jesus Christ does for everyone of His children. John tells us that it is God's desire that we do not go on sinning but IF we do, we have someone who will be a stand between the Father and our sin, and it is Jesus.

When we put our trust in Jesus and are saved, He becomes our advocate. When we are in court, an advocate provides support and advice for us and pleads our case to the judge. Advocates know how to navigate complicated legal situations with tact and depth of knowledge. Jesus is not only good at supporting our case, but He is the **BEST** at it. When we think of how grateful we can be as Christians, this truth is at the very top because without Jesus and His advocating work, we all would be captured in our sins. Thankful we can be declared "not guilty."

Gratitude Corner. Tell God what you are thinking and feeling based on what you have discovered in this reading. Tell someone else about it too. Remember you are in the "Import/Export" business/ministry.

<u>**Applications** to **"God ADVOCATES for me"** and scriptural support:</u>

- *God advocates for me and therefore I can fully follow His advice in His Word. (Jn. 14:16,26; 15:26; 16:7)*
- *God advocates for me and therefore He understands what I am going through. (Heb. 4:15-16)*

God is JOY for me....

"You have shown me the way of life, and you will fill me with the joy of your presence." -Acts 2:28

Joy is essential to the Christian life. The Scriptures are clear: God's people are both commanded to rejoice and characterized by rejoicing. Biblical joy can be defined as choosing to respond to external circumstances with inner contentment and satisfaction, because we know that God will use these experiences to accomplish His work in and through our lives. But here's the deal with JOY. Christ is the source of all joy and He is actually JOY for you. It is a fruit of the Spirit. (Gal. 5:22) The joy of Jesus is not a joy that comes and goes but is constant and intimate.

Joe Scriven came from Ireland to be a missionary to the Iroquois Indians more than 100 years ago. He left his fiancé in Ireland, and when she finally sailed across the ocean, she was killed in a tragic accident. Here was a man who loved God, who had to bury his fiancé with his own hands. A year later, he wrote a letter home to his mother with these words that we love to sing: "What a friend we have in Jesus, all our sins and griefs to bear. What a privilege to carry everything to God in prayer. Have we trials and temptations? Is there trouble anywhere? We should never be discouraged. Take it to the Lord in prayer." That's exactly what we must learn to do.

Gratitude Corner. Tell God what you are thinking and feeling based on what you have discovered in this reading. Tell someone else about it too. Remember you are in the "Import/Export" business/ministry.

<u>Applications</u> to "**God is JOY for me**" and scriptural support:

- *God gives us joy as we trust Him and believe in Him on a daily basis. (I Pet. 1:8-9)*
- *God gives us joy and it is our strength. (Nehemiah 8:10)*
- *God gives us joy because we come to the full knowledge of what He has done for us. (Is. 35:10)*

God SENDS me....

So, Jesus said to them again, "Peace be with you; as the Father has sent Me, I also send you." -John 20:21

To be sent to speak on behalf of a country or its country's chief leader is indeed a great honor and responsibility. An ambassador or an envoy has the extreme privilege of representing the country they are a part of and a country they love. If you are God's child, that is your divine work and privilege every day of your life. To represent the greatest Leader in the whole word, Christ. To represent the power and call of Heaven itself. And to share its clear and lifechanging message with all those who are in your sphere of influence. It doesn't get any more important than that.

Just as Jesus was sent by the Father, so we have been sent. (Rom. 10:14-17) How grateful we can be that God in Christ has given us such a lofty position and purpose in this world. The word for **"send"** is an interesting word. It means to be – *put forth and permitted to go.* You, by the grace and authority of Christ, have been cast forth into this dark culture to bring the light of the glory of God in the face of Jesus Christ. Have you answered the call to bear witness of the one who has freed us from darkness into His marvelous light? I hope so but one thing is for sure. We can be eternally thankful for the job Christ has given us 24/7, 365! Can I hear an Amen?

Gratitude Corner. Tell God what you are thinking and feeling based on what you have discovered in this reading. Tell someone else about it too. Remember you are in the "Import/Export" business/ministry.

Applications to "God SENDS me" and scriptural support:

- *God sends us into the world as Jesus' representative. (Jn. 17:18)*
- *God sends us into the world to proclaim the good news of salvation. (2 Cor. 4:5)*
- *God sends us into this world as ambassadors for Christ. (2 Cor. 5:14-21)*

God PRAYS for me....

"And he who searches our hearts knows the mind of the Spirit, because the Spirit intercedes for the saints in accordance with God's will" -Romans 8:27

Somebody is always praying for you 24/7 - 365. Isn't that great news? Sometimes we feel alone, and we believe that not many really care for us or even remember us before the throne of God. But there is Someone who constantly prays for you in accordance with the will of God and that is Jesus Christ through the person of the Holy Spirit. Now if Jesus is praying for us, could we be in any better position to perform the will of God than in that sweet spot? Jesus is interceding for you now – today. Are you at the end of your rope? Are you dealing with a diagnosis that is unfavorable? Are you feeling like you don't have a friend? Are you about to throw the towel in and leave the fold? Don't be dismayed? Jesus is for you and who can be against you.

Hebrews 7:25 says, *"He is able, once and forever, to save those who come to God through him. He lives forever to intercede with God on their behalf"* (NLT). And Romans 8:34 says, *"It is Christ who died, and furthermore is also risen, who is even at the right hand of God, who also makes intercession for us"* (NKJV). Robert Murray M'Cheyne, a 19th-century Scottish minister, said, *"If I could hear Christ praying for me in the next room, I would not fear a million enemies. Yet the distance makes no difference; he is praying for me!"* Amen? Never again feel like no one cares. The One who made it all and sustains it, is praying for you and that makes it all good.

Gratitude Corner. Tell God what you are thinking and feeling based on what you have discovered in this reading. Tell someone else about it too. Remember you are in the "Import/Export" business/ministry.

<u>Applications</u> to "**God PRAYS for me**" and scriptural support:

- *God is praying for you everyday and all day and His prayers will be answered. (Rom. 8:34; Heb. 7:25)*

God is all we NEED....

The tried and true statement is what we need to hear on this last reminder of how thankful we can and should be because of God's work done for us and in us. Here it is: **"You don't know how much you need the Lord until He is all you have."** We have all been there. But I wonder how often we remind ourselves that those of us who are God's children by the new birth are privileged people beyond all of the masses of men and women across the globe. We can understand what it means to be fully shipwrecked on God and His Son, Jesus Christ. We can grasp the need we have for God in our lives and without Him, we know what kind of mess we would be in.

Do you believe that God is truly enough for you at the end of the day? If not, why not? Even Peter, who was accustomed to putting his foot in his mouth, understood that Jesus was enough and that there was **NO ONE ELSE** that could do for him and humanity what He could do. He said, *"where else can we go? For you have the words of eternal life."* We can say the same and we know that because of this declaration, we can be grateful and thankful the rest of our days. That is the crux of this book that you just got done reading. Blessings. (Eph. 1:3)

Gratitude Corner. Tell God what you are thinking and feeling based on what you have discovered in this reading. Tell someone else about it too. Remember you are in the "Import/Export" business/ministry.

How Should We Then Live?

The Healing Power of Gratitude. It truly is a healing balm for the believer in Christ. I am reminded every day that if Jesus never did another thing for us by way of blessing, His work on the cross applied to our sinful heart – **is more than enough.** We are so contrary as to how we view God and talk to Him. He has called us, saved us and secured us and we often live like we are heading toward an uncertain future. But when we understand what God has truly done for us in Christ and we fully grasp all that He has promised for us not only NOW but in ETERNITY, we cannot avoid the pleasant posture of divine gratitude and joy.

One of my favorite passages of scripture from the feeble hands of the apostle Paul is found in Titus 2:11-14. It reads, *"For the grace of God has appeared that offers salvation to all people. It teaches us to say "No" to ungodliness and worldly passions, and to live self-controlled, upright and godly lives in this present age, while we wait for the blessed hope-the appearing of the glory of our great God and Savior, Jesus Christ, who gave himself for us to redeem us from all wickedness and to purify for himself a people that are his very own, eager to do what is good."* What a hope and a promise that God gives us about how to live – and how to someday day and the joys that await us.

Share this book with others. Read it through again sometime in the future. Remind yourself regularly that you are what you are – by the grace of God. A Christian, who is among the happiest people on the planet!

Chris J. Gregas

Other Books From Chris J. Gregas

All available on Amazon.com

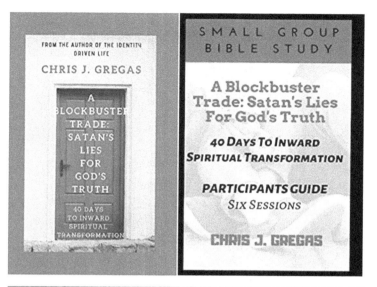
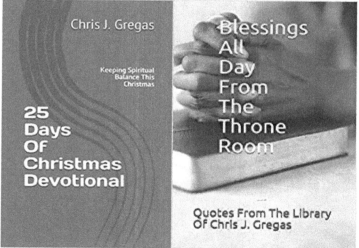

You can reach Chris @ ***chrisjgregas@gmail.com*** for any spiritual help you may need or to have him come and speak to your group or church. He is also available to interview or be counseled from. Thanks.

Printed in the USA
CPSIA information can be obtained
at www.ICGtesting.com
LVHW092018041224
798230LV00004B/508